Exploring Cultures
in the Kitch[en]

Chinese Culture and Cooking

Lindsey Lowe

Cavendish
Square

Published in 2024 by Cavendish Square Publishing, LLC
2544 Clinton Street, Buffalo, NY 14224

Portions of this work were originally authored by Tracey Kelly and published as *The Culture and Recipes of China*. All new material this edition authored by Lindsey Lowe.

Website: cavendishsq.com

This publication represents the opinions and views of the author based on his or her personal experience, knowledge, and research. The information in this book serves as a general guide only. The author and publisher have used their best efforts in preparing this book and disclaim liability rising directly or indirectly from the use and application of this book.

All websites were available and accurate when this book was sent to press.

Children's Publisher: Anne O'Daly
Design Manager: Keith Davis
Picture Manager: Sophie Mortimer

Picture Credits
t=top, c=center, b=bottom, l=left, r=right
Front Cover: Shutterstock: mokokomo br, Saigoneer tl; Thinkstock: RClassenLayouts bl.
Interior: Dreamstime: Chuyu 7, Fike2308 38-39c, Vladimir Grigorev 36-37t, Ravindran John Smith 28, Szefei 30b, Ray Woo 10; iStock: g01xm 9, SolStock 38-39t; Shutterstock: 25, 29br, ABCDstock 5t, Johannes Bluemel 21, Silvia Bogdanski 43, Norman Chan 15b, CW pix 8-9t, Olga Danylenko 6b, D N Davis 37, Elena11 31, ESB Professional 5b, Svilen G 6t, Jiang Hongyan 23b, Jono Photography 22, Dmitry Kalinovsky 10-11b, Kim Kuperkova 11, Jianbing Lee 39, Mcimage 30t, Zen S Prarom 22-23t, Shaun Robinson 28-29t, saravutpics 8b, Alen Thien 20-21, vkuslandia 45, Naruedom Yaempongsa 4, Jimmy Yan 36-37b; Thinkstock: Matt Image 1l, RClassenLayouts 35b.

Special thanks to Klaus Arras for all other photography.

Cataloging-in-Publication Data

Names: Lowe, Lindsey.
Title: Chinese culture and cooking / Lindsey Lowe.
Description: Buffalo, New York : Cavendish Square Publishing, 2024. | Series: Exploring cultures in the kitchen | Includes glossary and index.
Identifiers: ISBN 9781502668950 (pbk.) | ISBN 9781502668967 (library bound) | ISBN 9781502668974 (ebook)
Subjects: LCSH: Cooking, Chinese--Juvenile literature. | Food habits--China--Juvenile literature. | China--Social life and customs--Juvenile literature.
Classification: LCC TX724.5.C5 O34 2024 | DDC 641.5951--dc23

CPSIA compliance information: Batch #CSCSQ24: For further information contact Cavendish Square Publishing LLC at 1-877-980-4450.

Printed in the United States of America

Find us on

Contents

Spotlight on China

China is a big country. One-third of the land area is mountains. About one-third of its 1.4 billion people live in cities. The rest live in the country. Delicious food has been on Chinese menus for thousands of years!

China is a huge country in east Asia. It is bordered by 14 other countries.

Rice is a staple food in China. It is served with vegetables, meat, or fish.

Long Live China!

China is a land of diverse ethnic cultures. Officially known as the People's Republic of China, the nation has many neighbors. It is bordered by India, Pakistan, Afghanistan, Tajikistan, Kyrgyzstan, Kazakhstan, Mongolia, Russia, North Korea, Vietnam, Laos, Myanmar, Bhutan, and Nepal. The landscapes in China range from stunning mountains and rolling hills to tranquil plains and arid deserts. Its crowded cities are packed with people and skyscrapers. China's ancient civilizations developed some of the world's key technologies, such as papermaking, printing, silk manufacturing, and the invention of the compass. Its delicious cuisine is also legendary. Wansui China (long live China)!

The Great Wall of China in the north of the country runs for over 13,000 miles (21,000 km) from east to west. It dates back to 210 BCE.

RUSSIA

MONGOLIA

XINJIANG

Great Wall of China

Beijing

CHINA

Huang He (Yellow River)

Shanghai

PACIFIC OCEAN

XIZANG

SICHUAN

Yangtze River

NEPAL

INDIA

Hong Kong

MYANMAR

LAOS

PACIFIC OCEAN

VIETNAM

Hong Kong is a business center and the wealthiest Chinese city. It was ruled by the British from 1841–1997.

Landscapes

Most people live in the fertile green plains of eastern China and along the coast. Other landscapes include karsts—unique limestone formations that thrust up out of the ground. The South China Karst covers 193,000 square miles (500,000 square km). China has many vast deserts, too. The Taklimakan is the largest in the country, covering 130,000 square miles (337,600 square km). Its massive, shifting sand dunes can reach heights of up to 1,000 feet (300 m)!

Karst rock formations tower over the trees in Stone Forest Park, in Kunming, Yunnan Province.

Mighty Mountains

China is home to some huge mountain ranges. They take up about one-third of the country's land area. In the southwest, the majestic Himalayas rise in jagged, snow-capped peaks along the border. They include the world's tallest mountain, Mount Everest, at 29,035 feet (8,849 m). Climbers from all over the world come to scale its peak. Other ranges include the Kunlun, Tian Shan, Qinling, and Taihang Mountains.

The Himalayas sit on the border between Nepal and Xizang Province, or Tibet.

Powerful Rivers

China has some of the mightiest rivers on Earth. The Yangtze (meaning "long river"), at 3,915 miles (6,300 km), is the longest river in the country and the third-longest in the world. It flows through an amazing range of scenery, from high mountain peaks to inland plains and jungles. It also flows through five major cities and the Three Gorges Dam, the world's largest dam. Many towns were flooded to build the dam, which was created to irrigate crops and generate power. The Yellow River, or Huang He, is the second-longest river in China at 3,398 miles (5,464 km) long. It is called the "Cradle of Chinese Civilization," as the first Chinese cultures grew up along its banks. In the summer, heavy rains sometimes cause dangerous floods. Over the years, millions of people have died in floods.

DID YOU KNOW?

The giant panda is the national symbol of China. This gentle giant is native to the mountains of central China. It lives mostly on bamboo shoots. The panda is a threatened species. There are only about 1,864 left in the wild.

The Yangtze River cuts through green mountains in Yunnan Province, in the southwest of China.

Food and Agriculture

Only a small percentage of China is good for farming. Some foods are imported to feed the huge population. Fertile areas are used to raise animals and to grow rice, fruits, and vegetables.

Growing Rice

Rice is a universal food in China and is eaten with almost every meal. The wet, warm south and the center of China produce the most rice. There are some large farms, but much of it is grown on small farms just outside the villages. Every square inch of fertile land is used. In hilly places, farmers build level platforms called terraces to grow rice. Rainwater that runs off the hillsides is collected and guided into the terraces to water the plants. The water forms glistening pools in these paddies, or rice fields. Rice growing is time-consuming. Growers plant seedlings in the paddies by hand, and the rice is harvested by hand, too.

Watered rice terraces glisten in the sun.

A traditional fisherman with the cormorants he uses to catch fish on the Li River.

First-Class Fishing

With around 9,000 miles (14,500 km) of coastline, China has access to a lot of fishing. Its fishing industry is gigantic, producing around 62 million tons (56 million metric tons) of fish and seafood per year. This is used both to feed China's people and to export (sell) to other countries. Fishermen catch crabs, shrimp, and octopus, as well as mackerel, herring, flounder, sardines, sharks, and anchovies. Freshwater fish are caught in China's lakes and rivers. These include catfish, rainbow trout, salmon, whitebait, mullet, carp, bream, and eel. Many different types of seaweed and algae are collected for food, too.

DID YOU KNOW?

China is the world's top producer of crops such as corn, wheat, peanuts, and soybeans. It is also number one in rice growing and export. So the rice on your plate probably comes from China!

Different kinds of fish are sold in a market in Hong Kong. Chinese cuisine uses a wide variety of fresh fish and seafood.

Colorful fields make up the dramatic landscape in Yunnan Province, southwest China.

Fertile Farmland

China's farmlands produce large crops of wheat, corn, and millet in the north. Sweet potatoes, peanuts, and oilseeds—such as sesame, sunflower, and rapeseed—are other important crops. Soybeans are grown to make cooking oil as well as soy milk and tofu, a protein-rich ingredient used in many Chinese dishes. Green and jasmine tea plantations provide China with its favorite drink, while black tea is grown for export. Spice crops, such as chile, ginger, star anise, and Sichuan peppercorns, are used in the famously spicy Sichuan cuisine.

Fruitful Orchards

Chinese orchards produce apples, pears, and grapes by the thousands of tons, and much of this fruit is sold for export. The country also produces mangoes, bananas, and other tropical fruits. These grow well in Guangzhou, formerly Canton, northwest of Hong Kong. Lychee, a delicious, delicate-tasting fruit with white flesh, also grows in the region. Citrus fruit is grown across the warm south of China, especially oranges, mandarins, and pomelos, which have a thick yellow or green skin and taste a little like grapefruit.

Lychee, or litchi, is a favorite fruit in China. When its rough skin is peeled, the fragrant white flesh is revealed.

Grassland Grazing

China raises huge numbers of livestock (animals). Cattle, sheep, and goats graze in the dry northern grasslands. In remote rural areas, nomadic people such as Mongolians raise sheep and goats as well as camels. Pork is the most common meat eaten in China, so there is a large pig population. Pigs are raised and processed mostly along the Yangtze River. Poultry, such as chicken, ducks, geese, ostriches, and quail, are raised in vast numbers to produce meat and eggs.

Asian cows graze in a meadow near the Li River, in the Guangxi region.

Let's Cook!

Cooking is a lot of fun! In this book, you will learn about different ingredients, which tastes go together, and new cooking methods. Some recipes have steps that you'll need help with, so you can ask a parent or another adult. When your delicious meal is ready, serve it up to family and friends!

Serves 4-6

This tells you how many people the meal will feed.

This lists all the ingredients you need for your meal.

YOU WILL NEED

* 5 ounces milk chocolate or semisweet chocolate (or half of each)
* 2 large eggs
* 2 tablespoons powdered sugar

Before you begin, check that you have everything. Get all the ingredients ready before you start cooking.

TOP TIP

You can choose any type of chocolate you like.

Top Tips give you more information about the recipe or the ingredients.

For many meals, you need to chop an onion. Cut a thin slice off at both ends, then pull off the papery skin. Cut the onion in half down the middle. Put one half, cut side down, on the cutting board. Hold it with one hand and cut slices with the other hand. Hold the slices together, then cut across them to make small cubes. Be careful not to cut yourself!

Some recipes use fresh chiles—and they are very hot! Chile seeds and the white pith make your skin burn, so always wear rubber or vinyl gloves when chopping chiles. If you don't have any gloves, wash your hands really well afterward, and do not touch your skin or eyes for a while. To chop, trim the chile stalk, then halve lengthwise. Scrape out the seeds and throw them away. Slice the stalk into fine pieces.

METRIC CONVERSIONS

Oven Temperature	
°F	°C
275	140
300	150
325	170
350	180
375	190
400	200
425	220
450	230
475	240

Liquid	
cups	milliliters
¼	60
½	120
¾	180
1	240

Weight	
ounces	grams
1	30
2	60
3	85
4	115
5	140
6	175
7	200
8	225

Sugar	
cups	grams
¼	50
½	100
¾	150
1	200

Flour	
cups	grams
¼	30
½	60
¾	90
1	120

Egg-Fried Rice

Serves 4

Fried rice is eaten daily in northern China. It is delicious on its own, but you can add vegetables, shrimp, or pork to give variety to the dish.

YOU WILL NEED

* ✳ 2¼ cups white rice
* ✳ 4 eggs, beaten
* ✳ light soy sauce
* ✳ 2 scallions
* ✳ ⅓ cup peeled shrimp
* ✳ ⅓ cup ham
* ✳ 4 tablespoons soybean oil or other vegetable oil
* ✳ ⅓ cup cooked green peas

TOP TIP

Always store any unused, cooked rice in the refrigerator and use it within one day. Reheat it until it is piping hot to kill bacteria.

1 Measure the rice and place in a saucepan. Add 3 ⅓ cups water, and let the rice swell up. Discard some water, leaving ½ inch (1 cm) above the level of the rice. Put the saucepan on the heat and bring to a boil, then turn down the heat and simmer.

2 Wrap the saucepan lid in a clean dishcloth and put it back on the saucepan. Make sure the dishcloth is not hanging over the edge. Cook the rice for 10 minutes, without removing the lid or stirring. Take the pan off the heat. Remove the lid and leave the rice to cool for 45 minutes.

3 Crack the eggs into a bowl and stir in 2 tablespoons soy sauce. Trim the scallions. Then chop the scallions, shrimp, and ham into small pieces.

4 In a wok or other large pan, heat 2 teaspoons of the oil until sizzling. Add half the egg and soy sauce mixture, and cook it until it is set. It should look like an omelet. Remove, and cook the rest of the egg mixture.

5 Cut the two "omelets" into thin strips. Heat the rest of the oil in the wok and add the chopped scallions, shrimp, and ham. Stir-fry for 1–2 minutes, using a wooden spoon. Add the cooked rice and fry for 2 minutes. Finally, add the peas, and stir-fry for 2 more minutes. Stir in the omelet strips. Serve in bowls, with a small bowl of soy sauce on the side.

Crispy Greens

Serves 4

This recipe is usually made with bok choy, a type of Chinese cabbage, but you can use any cabbage or edible seaweed if you can find it at the store! The dish is yummy served with a stir-fry.

YOU WILL NEED

* ✱ 1 pound of bok choy leaves (or seaweed or cabbage)
* ✱ canola oil for frying
* ✱ ½–1 teaspoon salt
* ✱ 2 teaspoons sugar
* ✱ 3 tablespoons peanuts, pine nuts, or flaked almonds

1 Separate the bok choy leaves and wash them. Cut off the stems and throw them away. Pat the leaves dry with paper towels. Place a few of the leaves on top of each other. Holding them steady, cut into thin strips with a sharp knife. Then spread the strips out to dry for about 1 hour.

TOP TIP

If you can't get bok choy, use seaweed, but check that it is an edible variety. You can use any kind of cabbage instead.

3 Put a handful of the bok choy strips into the oil and fry them for 45 seconds. Count or keep looking at the clock—45 seconds is not very long! The leaves should turn dark green but should not burn.

4 Using a slotted spoon, lift the fried leaves out. Drain them on paper towels so the oil can run off. Put the drained leaves into a bowl, and put them in an oven preheated to 180°F to keep warm. Fry the rest of the leaves.

2 Turn on the burner and add about 2 tablespoons of oil to a wok. To check that the oil is hot enough, hold a wooden spatula in the oil. If bubbles appear right away, the oil is hot enough.

5 When all the leaves are fried, sprinkle them with the salt and sugar. Chop the peanuts, pine nuts, or almonds into little pieces. Sprinkle them over the top of the warm bok choy and serve.

Bang-Bang Chicken

Serves 4

This moist chicken dish gets its name from the sound of a chef tenderizing (softening) chicken breasts with a mallet—bang-bang!

YOU WILL NEED

* ✳ 4¼ cups chicken stock
* ✳ 4 boneless, skinless chicken breasts
* ✳ 3 ounces rice noodles, broken into short pieces
* ✳ 1 cucumber
* ✳ 1 tomato
* ✳ 2 scallions
* ✳ roasted sesame seeds
* ✳ ground Sichuan pepper

FOR THE SAUCE

* ✳ 3 ounces smooth, unsweetened peanut butter
* ✳ 3 garlic cloves
* ✳ 1 chile
* ✳ 3 tablespoons light soy sauce
* ✳ 1 handful fresh cilantro
* ✳ 1 tablespoon brown sugar
* ✳ 1 tablespoon rice vinegar
* ✳ 2 tablespoons sesame oil

1 Put the stock in a saucepan and bring to a boil. Add the chicken breasts and turn the heat down low. Simmer for about 15 minutes. Lift the chicken breasts out with a slotted spoon and let them cool. Slice the chicken into thin strips.

2 Put the rice noodles in a medium-size bowl. Boil some water and pour it over the noodles to cover. Let the noodles soak for about 5 minutes, then drain using a colander.

DID YOU KNOW?

Although it looks like other peppercorns, Sichuan pepper is not really a pepper. It is the red or pink berry of a tree, and it tastes lemony— and hot! It can make your mouth tingle.

3 Peel the cucumber and cut it in half lengthwise. Using a teaspoon, scrape out the seeds and discard them. Cut the halves into thin slices. Slice the tomato. Trim the scallions and slice them into rings.

4 Measure out all the sauce ingredients and put in a bowl. Blend them with a hand blender or in a mixer.

5 Put the noodles on a serving dish. Put the vegetables around the edge, and place the chicken slices on top. Sprinkle with sesame seeds and a tiny bit of Sichuan pepper over the top. Serve with the sauce.

National Celebrations

Festivals in China follow the lunar calendar, a calendar based on the cycles of the moon. There are many national and regional celebrations.

Chinese New Year

The New Year festival is the most important holiday in China. It usually falls between January 21 and February 20, depending on when the first new moon of the year appears in the sky. The festival lasts for 15 days. In the days before the festival, people clean their houses and get rid of old things to make room for a fresh start. They buy new clothes, especially for children. Paper cutouts made using red paper with the symbol *fu*, which means "happiness," are displayed in windows. During the festival, families and friends from across the country get together and have a big "reunion" feast. They eat special dumplings called *yuanbao*, as well as fish and a rice cake called New Year Cake. Families watch parades that feature lion dancing, where people dress in giant lion costumes. The dance is believed to bring good luck.

Two people dance inside a lion costume. The lion dance is part of the 15-day New Year Festival.

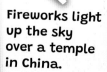

Fireworks light up the sky over a temple in China.

Festive Fireworks

Fireworks are thought to have been invented by mistake about 2,000 years ago when a cook mixed three ingredients together and they exploded when heated! People began to stuff hollow bamboo sticks with this substance, called gunpowder. When the sticks were lit, they shot into the air, and the first firecrackers were born. Fireworks are an essential part of Chinese celebrations. The loud bang they make is said to scare away evil spirits. Over the years, displays have become more and more sophisticated, with beautiful colors and designs. Each year, there are competitions to create new ones.

DID YOU KNOW?

Fireworks festivals spread from China across the world to Europe and America. The first American Independence Day fireworks were set off in Philadelphia on July 4, 1777.

Lantern Festival

The Lantern Festival ends on the 15th day of the Chinese New Year festival. The holiday began 2,000 years ago, but no one is really sure why. Today, people light lanterns hung with riddles for people to solve. They are often red for good luck. Fireworks are set off, and parades take place with beating drums, music, and lion dancing. Family and friends gather and share *yuanxiao*. This is a round rice ball with a filling made from sugar and ingredients such as walnuts, bean paste, and rose petals. People also look for a new love during the Lantern Festival. It is the Chinese equivalent of Valentine's Day!

Lanterns hang at the Wuhou Temple in Chengdu during the Lantern Festival.

Dragon Boat Race

The Dragon Boat Festival is a colorful holiday that takes place in June. It honors the politician and poet Qu Yuan (340–278 BCE), who was sent into exile by the king. Qu Yuan wrote poems about his love for China, then drowned himself in a river rather than see bad people control China. People jumped in boats and threw *zongzi*, sticky rice dumplings, into the water to keep the fish from eating Qu Yuan's body. Today, people watch thrilling dragon boat races across the country and make and eat zongzi.

People race boats during the Dragon Boat Festival in Hong Kong.

Moon Festival

The Mid-Autumn or Moon Festival is a holiday where people give thanks to the moon to celebrate the harvest. It takes place on the first full moon after the autumn equinox, usually in late September. People spend the evening outside, looking at the bright full moon. They eat moon cakes—special cakes made of pastry stuffed with bean paste. The cakes are round to symbolize the reunion of family and friends. People also take time to remember those who are far away.

Moon cakes stamped with striking designs are served with tea during the Moon Festival.

Pork Dumplings

Makes 25

"Yuanbao" is the word for a kind of money. Yunbao dumplings are made to look like money because this is believed to bring wealth to the people who eat them.

YOU WILL NEED

* 1 pack deep-frozen round wonton dough disks, 3 inches (7.5 cm) wide
* 2 ounces canned bamboo shoots
* 1 handful fresh cilantro
* 2 tender scallions
* ½ pound ground pork
* 1 garlic clove
* 1 teaspoon freshly grated ginger
* 1 tablespoon dark soy sauce
* 1 tablespoon sesame oil

PLUS

* canola oil for frying
* salad leaves, to garnish

1 Defrost the wonton circles overnight. Drain the can of bamboo shoots in a colander. Slice the bamboo shoots, cilantro, and scallions into small chunks.

2 Put the ground pork in a large bowl and crush the garlic into it. Add the grated ginger, soy sauce, and sesame oil. Wash your hands well, then knead all the ingredients together.

3 Put some cold water in a small bowl. Take a wonton and moisten its edges with water. Place 1 teaspoon of filling in the middle, and repeat with the other wontons.

4 Fold over the dough circles to make half circles. Then, using your fingers, press the edges of the pockets together to form a wavy rim. Flatten the dumpling slightly.

5 In a large skillet, heat 1 inch (2.5 cm) of canola oil. Put a few wontons in the pan and fry them for 3 minutes. Carefully flip them with a wooden spoon and fry the other sides for 3 minutes. Repeat until all the wontons have been fried. Serve on a platter on a bed of salad leaves.

DID YOU KNOW?

Dumplings are eaten at New Year parties. However, they are made beforehand, as knives are thought to bring bad luck.

Moon Cakes

Makes 12 cakes

Traditionally, people make these little cakes for the Moon Festival. They are eaten with family and friends while admiring the first full moon after the fall equinox.

YOU WILL NEED

* ✱ 3¼ cups self-rising flour
* ✱ 3 teaspoons baking powder
* ✱ ⅔ cup sugar
* ✱ ¾ cup vegetable oil
* ✱ 3 eggs, cracked into a bowl and lightly beaten
* ✱ about ⅔ cup cold water
* ✱ roasted sesame seeds
* ✱ about 1 pound sweet red bean paste

PLUS

* ✱ oil or butter for greasing the muffin pan
* ✱ 1 egg, cracked into a bowl and beaten, for brushing
* ✱ parsley, to garnish

1 Sift the flour and baking powder into a large bowl through a sieve to get rid of lumps. Add the sugar, oil, eggs, and water, and mix everything together with your hands (make sure you wash them first!). If you need to, add a little more water until the dough holds together in a ball but is not too sticky.

2 Using waxed paper, grease the holes in a muffin pan with a little oil or butter. Dust the work area with flour, and make a tennis ball-size piece of dough. Roll it out using a rolling pin to make a 4-inch (10 cm) circle.

3 Repeat, placing each circle in a hollow of the muffin pan so that it overhangs. Put 1 tablespoon bean paste in each one. Brush the pastry edges with a little water.

4 Heat the oven to 400°F. Make 12 walnut-size balls of dough and roll them out to make 2–3 inch (5–7.5 cm) circles. Place the smaller circles over the paste to make a "lid." Gently press all around the edges to enclose the paste.

5 Brush the tops with a little beaten egg, and bake in the oven for 25 minutes. Remove, leave to cool, and serve with a parsley garnish.

DID YOU KNOW

Moon cakes are often made in special molds with Chinese designs and characters on top!

Family Celebrations

Important occasions need careful planning. Sometimes Chinese people use astrology and fortune-tellers to help them pick an auspicious, or favorable, date.

Wedding Rituals

When two people marry in China, their families are joined together! This makes the choice of a wife or husband very important. Traditionally, the parents of a young man consult a fortune-teller to make sure that the bride and groom's personalities will be compatible. The fortune-teller is also asked to choose an auspicious wedding day. Many Chinese wear traditional red wedding clothes, but some brides wear Western-style white dresses. Brides wear new shoes for good luck. There is a huge banquet that may include fish, roast pork, lobster, and chicken. Each dish has a special meaning. For dessert, a wedding cake, which is called a "double happiness cake," is served.

A young Chinese couple wear traditional wedding outfits. Red is the color of happiness and marriage.

People arrive at a Buddhist temple in Beijing to burn incense and pray. Buddhism is one of China's major belief systems.

Religion and Beliefs

With 56 different ethnic groups in China, many religions have been practiced since ancient times. Folk religion, which shows respect for nature, ancestors, and local deities, is practiced by around 80 percent of Chinese people. It is mixed in with elements of Taoism and Confucianism, which give wise words about morals and the best way to behave. It is also mixed with Buddhism, which was introduced to China around 2,000 years ago. A small number of people practice Christianity and Islam.

DID YOU KNOW?

In the Chinese zodiac, each year is named after an animal. A person is thought to have the same traits as that animal. So people born in the Year of the Dragon are said to be energetic and feisty.

The Chinese zodiac repeats its cycle every 12 years. Find the year you were born to see your animal sign!

Birthdays

Thirty days after a Chinese baby is born, his or her birthday is celebrated. A special religious ceremony is held to let the ancestors know that a new child has arrived. Family and friends attend a banquet given by the parents, and red eggs are given to the guests. (Red is the color of happiness, and an egg symbolizes new life.) People give gifts and *hong bao*, or money wrapped in red and gold paper. The first birthday is also an important celebration. Traditionally, birthdays are then noted every 10 years, but today some celebrate every year.

The 60th birthday is important, as it is thought to be a big life milestone. Children host parties for their parents, giving them gifts and hong bao . Celebrations at 70, 80, and 90 years are even bigger occasions!

A daughter gives her mother a birthday gift wrapped in red and gold.

Taking Tea

People have been drinking tea in China for more than 4,000 years. Tea was first used as an herbal medicine to cure sickness and, later, as a religious offering. Eventually, tea was also drunk as a beverage. Buddhist monks brought a spiritual approach to tea drinking that is still used today in the tea ceremony. Each action is performed thoughtfully and savored, from choosing and making the tea in special teapots to pouring, smelling, and tasting the tea.

A woman pours tea in a ceremony at a traditional Chinese teahouse.

All in the Name

Three days after birth, a newborn baby is given a name. In China, people believe that this name will influence the baby's future life. It could be something to do with nature, such as "flower" or "river," or a quality, such as "intelligence" or "beauty." Some people consult a fortune-teller to find the right name. Often, it is the aunts, uncles, or grandparents who choose a name, not the child's parents.

DID YOU KNOW?

In China, numbers are believed to have great meaning. For example, "nine" means "forever"—so people give wedding money gifts in nines! The number of birth is "three," so people use it when a new baby is born.

Fried Noodles

Serves 4

During Chinese New Year and birthday celebrations, people make "longevity" noodles. These are never cut or broken by the cook, and it is said that the longer they are, the longer you might live!

YOU WILL NEED

* ✳ 2 tablespoons dried shiitake mushrooms
* ✳ 4 ounces long, thin rice or egg flour noodles
* ✳ 1 bunch scallions
* ✳ 1 cup snow peas
* ✳ 1 cup cooked shrimp
* ✳ 4 tablespoons oil
* ✳ 4 garlic cloves, peeled
* ✳ 2 tablespoons rice vinegar
* ✳ 2 tablespoons oyster sauce
* ✳ 1 tablespoon sweet soy sauce
* ✳ 3 tablespoons light soy sauce
* ✳ fresh cilantro leaves

1 Rinse the shiitake mushrooms under cold water. Put them in a small bowl with warm water. Let them soak for 20 minutes until they plump up.

2 Place the noodles in a large bowl and pour boiling water on top of them. Let the noodles swell up for 5 minutes, or according to the instructions on the package. Wash the scallions, trim, and cut into thin, diagonal slices.

5 Heat the oil in a wok or skillet. Crush the garlic into the wok and fry for a few seconds. Mix in the scallions and the snow peas, and fry for 1 minute. Add the cooked shrimp and mushrooms. Stir-fry for 5 minutes.

6 In a small bowl, mix the rice vinegar, oyster sauce, and the two soy sauces. Add the sauce to the wok, stirring rapidly. Using a colander, drain the noodles and add to the wok. Stir-fry for 2–3 minutes. Sprinkle with cilantro leaves and serve.

3 Rinse the snow peas under cold water, and trim the ends off. Cut the peas into diagonal strips.

4 Wash the shrimp and pat them dry using a paper towel. Squeeze the water out of the mushrooms. Twist off the stalks and throw them away. Slice the tops into thin strips.

DID YOU KNOW?

Shiitake mushrooms are very healthy. Because of this, they are considered to be a symbol of a long life. They are also used in traditional Chinese medicine.

Fortune Cookies

Makes 18-20 cookies

These are fun and easy to make! Each cookie is baked with a slip of paper inside it that has a "fortune" written on it—a lucky number, phrase, or message.

YOU WILL NEED

* 2 egg whites
* a few drops of vanilla extract
* 1 pinch salt
* ½ cup plus 2 tablespoons all-purpose flour
* ½ cup sugar

1 Write fortunes on little slips of paper, 2 inches (5 cm) by ½ inch (1 cm). Draw 3-inch (7.5 cm) circles across two sheets of parchment paper, leaving plenty of space between the circles. Turn the papers upside down and lay them on two cookie sheets.

DID YOU KNOW?

Here are a few ideas for fortunes: ● Happy news is on its way to you. ● You will have lots of friends. ● Everything has beauty, but not everyone sees it—Confucius. ● You will get a good grade on your next test.

2 Preheat the oven to 400°F. Put the egg whites and the vanilla extract in a deep bowl. Whisk using a hand blender or mixer until they are foamy, but not stiff. Add the salt, flour, and sugar, a little at a time, stirring. Gently stir in 1 teaspoon of water.

3 Drop 1 teaspoon of the batter into the middle of each marked circle. Spread it out with the back of a spoon to cover the whole circle. It should be a thin layer.

4 Bake the cookies in the oven for 6 minutes, or until they are light brown at the edges but still pale in the middle. Remove them from the oven and carefully lift them off the cookie sheet with a spatula. Turn them over onto a lightly oiled cutting board.

5 Quickly place a fortune on each cookie. Then fold the circles gently in half so that they make half-moon shapes. Turn the ends toward the middle. Place the cookies on a baking sheet and let them cool completely.

Be happy.

Life in China

Manufacturing and technology have made China's large major cities wealthy. However, in rural areas, people still live simply. They live in small villages and farm the land using traditional methods that have been employed for centuries.

City Life

Life in Chinese cities is crowded and hectic. People work for major world industries and huge cities, such as the capital city Beijing, Shanghai, and Chongqing, have massive populations of 20 to 30 million people. The standard of living is much higher than it is in the country, with inexpensive restaurants, transportation, and leisure activities. Modern skyscrapers dot the skyline alongside palaces, temples, and structures, such as the Great Wall, that represent China's culture through thousands of years of dynasties, or ruling eras.

Shoppers crowd the streets at lunchtime in Guangzhou, an important commercial port in Guangdong Province, South China.

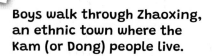
Boys walk through Zhaoxing, an ethnic town where the Kam (or Dong) people live.

Country Life

China's ethnic minority groups live all across the country. They make up many different cultures, so life in rural areas varies greatly. Around 45 percent of Chinese people live in small villages. Many live in courtyard houses without plumbing or appliances, and cows, pigs, and chickens share their space. Villagers work on nearby farms tending crops such as corn, wheat, and vegetables. Younger people often leave for jobs in the city, where they can earn three times more than in farm jobs. Then they send the money home to help their families make ends meet.

A Chinese farmer uses an ox to plow a field for planting in Guangxi region. Farmers still use traditional farming methods because tractors are expensive.

A Chinese family gathers to eat dinner together and share the day's news. They eat with chopsticks.

Going to School

Children in China must go to school for at least nine years. Their education is paid for by the government. Primary school starts at age 6 or 7, then children go to middle school from ages 12 to 15. High school continues for most students for three more years. Afterward, they may attend a university.

Classrooms are large—up to 50 children in each. Students have a very structured day. They start school at 8:00 a.m., when they raise the flag and sing the Chinese national anthem. Classes include math, computing, and Mandarin. English is now taught, too. During the break, everyone does exercises together, following moves as the gym teacher calls them out. After lunch in the cafeteria, classes continue until 4:00 p.m.

A large class of children studies at a school in Zibo, in the central Shandong Province.

Daily Menu

The Chinese start the day with one of many breakfast foods. They may have rice porridge (*congee*), dim sum dumplings, or a steamed bun (*bao*). Long, deep-fried dough sticks (*yóutiáo*) are popular, especially when dipped in a warm soy milk drink (*doujiang*). Lunch is often noodles or rice with meat or shrimp and vegetables. The whole family gathers for dinner, the largest meal of the day. Tasty dishes are placed on the table, and people help themselves to soup, fried rice, wontons, noodles, and meat and vegetable dishes.

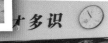

Rest and Play

Many people work six days a week in China, so they really enjoy their free time! Parks are popular and have playgrounds and free gym equipment. Concerts, dancing, and acrobatic displays may take place there as well. Favorite sports include badminton, table tennis, basketball, and volleyball. People of all ages practice *tai chi*, a martial art that uses slow and steady movements.

DID YOU KNOW?

Mandarin is China's official language. It is spoken by 70 percent of its people. Instead of letters and words, the written language has thousands of characters. Each represents a word and has a meaning of its own.

Student athletes race during a school track meet. Physical exercise is important in China.

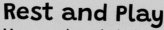

Deep-Fried Devils

Serves 4

These deep-fried fingers of bread dough make a delicious, crunchy snack. Try them for breakfast dipped in flavored milk or soy milk, the Chinese way!

YOU WILL NEED

* 1 loaf frozen bread dough
* plenty of neutral-tasting cooking oil, such as canola oil, for deep-frying

MAKE YOUR OWN DOUGH

Mix 1 package active dry yeast, ½ cup lukewarm water, and 1 teaspoon sugar. Cover and leave for a few minutes. Add another ½ cup water, 1 pound all-purpose flour, 4 tablespoons olive oil, and 1 teaspoon salt. Knead to make a smooth dough. Cover and leave to rise in the kitchen for 1 hour.

1 Wrap a dishcloth around the dough and let it defrost overnight in the refrigerator. Take the dough out about 1 hour before you are ready to make the deep-fried devils.

2 With clean hands, divide the dough into 24 equal pieces. Roll each piece between your hands to form a long sausage shape, and place on a baking sheet. Let the shapes rest for 1 hour at room temperature.

4 Pick up a "devil" with both hands. Pull it a little, then twist the ends in opposite directions as you pull. Very carefully place the twisted dough in the hot oil and fry until it is golden brown. Using a slotted spoon, carefully remove the devil, and drain it on paper towels. Repeat until all the devils are fried.

3 In a wok, heat 2 inches (5 cm) of oil for deep-frying. Sprinkle two drops of water into the oil. If it sizzles, the oil is hot enough.

Hot and Sour Soup

Serves 4

This classic soup is from Sichuan, in southern China. Tofu, chicken breast, bamboo shoots, and shiitake mushrooms are all spiced up with a garlic chile sauce!

YOU WILL NEED

* ✳ 4 dried shiitake mushrooms
* ✳ 6 ounces tofu
* ✳ 1 small can bamboo shoots (4 ounces)
* ✳ 5 ounces boneless, skinless chicken breast
* ✳ 5 cups chicken broth
* ✳ 2 tablespoons light soy sauce
* ✳ 2–3 tablespoons spicy garlic chile sauce
* ✳ 2 tablespoons cornstarch
* ✳ 2–3 tablespoons rice vinegar
* ✳ 1 egg, beaten
* ✳ 2 teaspoons sesame oil
* ✳ 1 scallion

1 Half-fill a bowl with warm water and add the mushrooms. Make sure they are covered. Soak them for 20 minutes.

TOP TIP

Try using tiger lily bud mushrooms in this soup instead of shiitake mushrooms. You can also use fresh chestnut mushrooms, but skip the soaking in step 1.

2 Drain the mushrooms, twist off the stalks, and throw them away. Slice the tops into thin strips. Chop the tofu, bamboo shoots, and chicken breast into small cubes.

4 Mix the cornstarch with a little cold water In a cup or mug. Slowly add this to the soup, stirring all the time. Then add the tofu and vinegar. Bring back to a boil. Now slowly drizzle in the beaten egg, which will form little lumps as it hits the hot soup. Drizzle the sesame oil on top. Trim and chop the scallion, sprinkle it over the soup, and serve.

3 Put the chicken broth in a saucepan. Add the soy sauce with the garlic chile sauce. Then add the mushrooms, bamboo shoots, and chicken. Turn the heat down low and simmer for 5 minutes.

DID YOU KNOW?

Tofu is a curd made from soybeans. It can be fried, baked, or broiled. Many Asian dishes use tofu because it is high in protein, making it good for vegetarians.

Fried Pork with Scallions

Serves 4

Stir-fries are easy to make—you just fry and stir! This recipe uses pork, but it can be made with any meat, fish, shrimp, or vegetables. Chile gives it a little kick!

YOU WILL NEED

* ✳ 6 tablespoons sweet soy sauce
* ✳ 8 tablespoons fish sauce
* ✳ 3 red chiles, trimmed and chopped
* ✳ 4 garlic cloves, peeled and chopped
* ✳ ⅔ cup vegetable stock
* ✳ 1½ teaspoons cornstarch
* ✳ 1 pound boneless pork chops
* ✳ 1 red and 1 green bell pepper
* ✳ 1–2 bunches scallions
* ✳ 4 tablespoons vegetable oil

1 Put the soy sauce, fish sauce, chiles, garlic, vegetable stock, and cornstarch in a small bowl. Stir well.

2 Using a sharp knife, cut the fat off the pork chops, then cut the meat into thin pieces. Put the pork in a bowl and add the soy sauce mixture. Turn the meat to make sure it is all coated. Put a clean dishcloth over the bowl. Leave to stand for 20 minutes.

3 Rinse the peppers and halve. Cut out the stalks, seeds, and white piths, and discard. Chop the flesh into small pieces. Rinse and trim the scallions, throwing away any yellow leaves. Slice the scallions into slanted rings.

5 Remove the pork from the soy sauce, but keep the liquid. Pat the meat dry. Place a few pieces at a time in the middle of the wok. Stir-fry for 2 minutes, then push to the edges and add more pieces. When all the meat is fried, stir it together. Add the soy sauce liquid. Stir-fry for 2–3 minutes. Put in individual bowls and serve.

4 Heat a wok. Add the oil, scallions, and peppers. Stir-fry for about 4 minutes.

TOP TIP

Fish sauce is made from fermented fish. It makes food taste salty, not fishy. If you can't find any fish sauce at the store, you can add a little salt instead.

Glossary

Chinese astrology A form of astrology where a person's birth year falls into one of 12 animal signs, each with different traits.

chopsticks A pair of sticks that make up the main eating utensil in China and other Asian countries. The sticks are held in one hand, between the thumb and the middle and forefingers. They are thinner at one end and can be made from bamboo, bone, metal, or plastic.

deities The gods or goddesses of any religion, or statues that represent them.

fish sauce A common ingredient in Asian dishes. It is made from fish but tastes mainly salty.

hong bao Small red envelopes containing money. They are given to children for Chinese New Year, for birthdays, or to brides and grooms at weddings.

karst A jagged landscape with limestone rock formations. The South China Karst is a World Heritage Site.

lunar month In China, a new month begins at midnight of the new moon (when it's not visible in the sky). The lunar calendar is used for deciding festival dates, for finding lucky dates for weddings, and for the zodiac.

moon cakes Little cakes made for the Moon Festival in the fall.

nomadic Describes people who have no permanent home but travel from place to place to find fresh grazing land for their livestock.

shiitake A type of Chinese mushroom. Other types include tiger lily buds and chestnut mushrooms.

Sichuan pepper A tangy berry that is used in many southern Chinese dishes. It leaves a tingly feeling in the mouth and tastes slightly lemony.

stir-frying A common method of cooking food in China and other Asian countries. Food is fried quickly in a very hot wok while the cook stirs it constantly.

tofu A curd made from soybeans. It is white and bland tasting, but it takes on the flavors of other foods. It is high in protein.

wok A bowl-shaped frying pan that is used for stir-frying food over high heat.

Further Resources

Books

Branscome, Allison.
All About China: Stories, Songs, Crafts and Games for Kids.
Tuttle Publishing, 2018.

Demuth, Patricia Brennan.
Where Is the Great Wall?
Penguin Workshop, 2015.

Hustad, Douglas.
Your Passport to China (World Passport).
Capstone Press, 2020.

Jenkins, Celia.
China: Travel for Kids: The Fun Way to Discover China.
Dinobibi Publishing, 2019.

Kampff, Joseph.
The Coolest Chinese Foods.
Rosen Publishing, 2023.

Walker, Cindy.
Chinese Holiday Foods.
Independently published, 2022.

Websites

kids.nationalgeographic.com/geography/countries/article/china
Introduction to China from National Geographic Kids.
kids.britannica.com/kids/article/China/345666
Page with facts and links to all things China.
www.kids-cooking-activities.com/Asian-cooking.html
Recipes and videos for young cooks.
www.china-family-adventure.com/chinese-culture.html
All about China, with fascinating pages on its history, geography, traditions, culture, and food.

Index